EDITORIAL

# IN THIS ISSUE:

## ISSUE 10 OCTOBER 2017

**PUBLISHER**
Tourism Tattler (Pty) Ltd.
PO Box 891, Umhlanga Rocks, 4320
KwaZulu-Natal, South Africa.
Website: www.tourismtattler.com

**EXECUTIVE EDITOR** Des Langkilde
Cell: +27 (0)82 374 7260
Fax: +27 (0)86 651 8080
E-mail: editor@tourismtattler.com
Skype: tourismtattler

**MAGAZINE ADVERTISING**
**ADVERTISING DIRECTOR** Bev Langkilde
Cell: +27 (0)71 224 9971
Fax: +27 (0)86 656 3860
E-mail: bev@tourismtattler.com
Skype: bevtourismtattler

**SUBSCRIPTIONS**
http://eepurl.com/bocIdD

**BACK ISSUES** (Click on the covers below).

## CONTENTS

### AFRICA: SUSTAINABLE TOURISM SOLUTIONS
- 06 Eco & Sustainable Tourism Icons
- 07 SSTL Joins #IY2017 Initiative
- 08 Why Join the Fair Trade Tourism?

### ACCOLADES
- 09 Celebrating the 2017 Lilizela Provincial Award Winners
- 10 Lilizela Tourism Awards 2017 Provincial Winners List

### BUSINESS & FINANCE
- 18 South African Tourism Statistics: Jan-Jun 2017
- 19 Tourism Business Index Half-Year Report 2017
- 20 Domestic Tourism: Trends & Opportunities
- 21 The Revenue Journey - Part 2: Navigating the Journey

### CONSERVATION
- 22 Kruger Park 2017 Rhino Census

### EVENTS
- 24 Bleisure Events: Africa's Saving Grace
- 25 Hotel App to be Launched at ITB Asia 2017

### HOSPITALITY
- 26 Floral Cuisine: Using Flowers in Cooking
- 28 The Business of Food Travel Podcast

### LEGAL
- 28 Social Media & Defamation - Part 2

### TRANSPORT
- 30 Vehicle Review: Mazda BT-50

### EDITORIAL CONTRIBUTORS
Alicia Giliomee — Lee-Anne Bac
Bonné de Bod — Louis Nel
Des Langkilde — Martin Janse van Vuuren
Elzaan van Rhyn — Tessa Buhrmann

### MAGAZINE SPONSORS
- 02 Kenya Tourism Board
- 05 World Luxury Hotel Awards
- 12 de Stijl Gariep Hotel
- 12 Beverley Country Cottages
- 12 Hamilton Parks Country Lodge
- 12 Petit & Grande Plaisir
- 13 Timbavati Safari Lodge
- 13 Belurana Collection
- 14 Kosmos Manor Guest House
- 14 River Place Manor
- 14 Big Sky Cottages
- 14 Thaba Tshwene Game Lodge
- 15 Bookings2Africa.com

### SUPPORTED CHARITIES
- 16 NSRI South Africa
- 32 Diabetes South Africa

▼ SEP 2017 ▼ AUG 2017 ▼ JUL 2017

▼ JUN 2017 ▼ MAY 2017 ▼ APR 2017
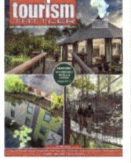

▼ MAR 2017 ▼ FEB 2017 ▼ JAN 2017

▼ DEC 2016 ▼ NOV 2016 ▼ OCT 2016

**Disclaimer:** The Tourism Tattler is published by Tourism Tattler (Pty) Ltd and is the official trade journal of various trade 'associations' (see page 02). The Tourism Tattler digital e-zine, is distributed free of charge to bona fide tourism stakeholders. Letters to the Editor are assumed intended for publication in whole or part and may therefore be used for such purpose. The information provided and opinions expressed in this publication are provided in good faith and do not necessarily represent the opinions of Tourism Tattler (Pty) Ltd, its 'Associations', its staff and its production suppliers. Advice provided herein should not be soley relied upon as each set of circumstances may differ. Professional advice should be sought in each instance. Neither Tourism Tattler (Pty) Ltd, its 'Associations', its staff and its production suppliers can be held legally liable in any way for damages of any kind whatsoever arising directly or indirectly from any facts or information provided or omitted in these pages or from any statements made or withheld or from supplied photographs or graphic images reproduced by the publication.

# Atta
### AFRICAN TRAVEL & TOURISM ASSOCIATION

## PROMOTING TOURISM TO
# AFRICA
### FROM ALL CORNERS OF THE WORLD

**Recognised as the Voice of African Tourism, Atta reaches across 22 countries in Africa, showcasing over 530 elite buyers and suppliers of African tourism product.**

- Leading role at trade shows around the world
- Networking opportunities
- Industry representation on international commitees & the media
- Interactive platform for information & education
- Daily news service on all aspects of African tourism
- Network of specialist consultants

**Join our knowledgeable and experienced membership to increase awareness and visibility of your company**

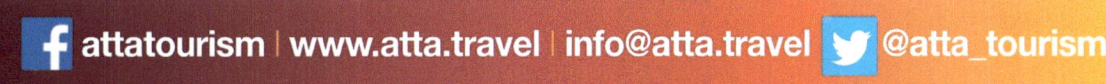

attatourism | www.atta.travel | info@atta.travel | @atta_tourism

**Lead Sponsor** | Working in partnership with Atta

**SOUTH AFRICAN AIRWAYS**
A STAR ALLIANCE MEMBER

# EDITORIAL
# ACCREDITATION

## Official Travel Trade Journal and Media Partner to:

**The Africa Travel Association (ATA)**
Tel: +1 212 447 1357 • Email: info@africatravelassociation.org • Website: www.africatravelassociation.org

ATA is a division of the Corporate Council on Africa (CCA), and a registered non-profit trade association in the USA, with headquarters in Washington, DC and chapters around the world. ATA is dedicated to promoting travel and tourism to Africa and strengthening intra-Africa partnerships. Established in 1975, ATA provides services to both the public and private sectors of the industry.

**The African Travel & Tourism Association (Atta)**
Tel: +44 20 7937 4408 • Email: info@atta.travel • Website: www.atta.travel

Members in 22 African countries and 37 worldwide use Atta to: Network and collaborate with peers in African tourism; Grow their online presence with a branded profile; Ask and answer specialist questions and give advice; and Attend key industry events.

**National Accommodation Association of South Africa (NAA-SA)**
Tel: +27 86 186 2272 • Fax: +2786 225 9858 • Website: www.naa-sa.co.za

The NAA-SA is a network of mainly smaller accommodation providers around South Africa – from B&Bs in country towns offering comfortable personal service to luxurious boutique city lodges with those extra special touches – you're sure to find a suitable place, and at the same time feel confident that your stay at an NAA-SA member's establishment will meet your requirements.

**Regional Tourism Organisation of Southern Africa (RETOSA)**
Tel: +27 11 315 2420/1 • Fax: +27 11 315 2422 • Website: www.retosa.co.za

RETOSA is a Southern African Development Community (SADC) institution responsible for tourism growth and development. RETOSA's aims are to increase tourist arrivals to the region through. RETOSA Member States are Angola, Botswana, DR Congo, Lesotho, Madagascar, Malawi, Mauritius, Mozambique, Namibia, Seychelles, South Africa, Swaziland, Tanzania, Zambia and Zimbabwe.

**Southern African Vehicle Rental and Leasing Association (SAVRALA)**
Contact: manager@savrala.co.za • Website: www.savrala.co.za

Founded in the 1970's, SAVRALA is the representative voice of Southern Africa's vehicle rental, leasing and fleet management sector. Our members have a combined national footprint with more than 600 branches countrywide. SAVRALA are instrumental in steering industry standards and continuously strive to protect both their members' interests, and those of the public, and are therefore widely respected within corporate and government sectors.

**Seychelles Hospitality & Tourism Association (SHTA)**
Tel: +248 432 5560 • Fax: +248 422 5718 • Website: www.shta.sc

The Seychelles Hospitality and Tourism Association was created in 2002 when the Seychelles Hotel Association merged with the Seychelles Hotel and Guesthouse Association. SHTA's primary focus is to unite all Seychelles tourism industry stakeholders under one association in order to be better prepared to defend the interest of the industry and its sustainability as the pillar of the country's economy.

**International Coalition of Tourism Partners (ICTP)**
Website: www.tourismpartners.org
ICTP is a travel and tourism coalition of global destinations committed to Quality Services and Green Growth.

**International Institute for Peace through Tourism**
Website: www.iipt.org
IIPT is dedicated to fostering tourism initiatives that contribute to international understanding and cooperation.

**ITB Asia 2017**
Website: www.itb-asia.com
25 to 27 October 2017 Marina Bay Sands®, Singapore.
ITB Asia is the leading B2B travel trade event for the entire Asia-Pacific region.

**Tourism, Hotel Investment and Networking Conference 2017**
Website: www.thincafrica..com
THINC Africa 2017 takes place in Cape Town, South Africa from 6-7 September.

**The Hotel Show Africa 2017**
Website: TheHotelShowAfrica.com
Thousands of hospitality professionals from around the world will be at Gallagher Convention Centre in Johannesburg from 25-27 June.

**The Safari Awards**
Website: www.safariawards.com
Safari Award finalists are amongst the top 3% in Africa and the winners are unquestionably the best.

**SHWTE 2017**
Website: SanganaiTourismExpo.com
27 Sep - 01 Oct at the Zimbabwe International Fair Grounds, Bulawayo.
The 2016 edition attracted: 212 Buyers, 236 Exhibitors, 3116 Meetings, and 5034 Connections.

"Africa's Premier Business Exchange"

**World Luxury Hotel Awards**
Website: www.luxuryhotelawards.com
World Luxury Hotel Awards is an international company that provides award recognition to the best hotels from all over the world.

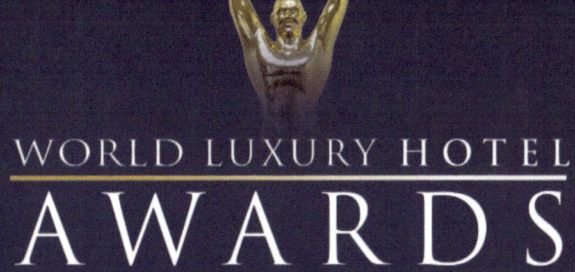

PARTNER — SPECIAL FEATURE — AFRICA'S SUSTAINABLE TOURISM GEMS

Launching Africa's sustainable tourism gems this month with a selection of South Africa's eco-friendly hotels and lodges, Tourism Tattler has partnered with Eco Atlas – an award winning eco-travel choice website. Where a featured eco-friendly property is already listed on Eco Atlas, we've shown the applicable icons.

## RESOURCE USE

 **Water Saving:** 3 or more of the following practices in place: a no-leak policy, water audit, flow restrictors on taps and shower heads, dual flush toilet cisterns, harvesting rain water, utilising waste water (grey water), only watering early morning and evening, alien tree removal, planting water wise, drip irrigation system, compost toilet, garden well mulched.

 **Energy Saving:** 3 or more of the following practices in place: energy A- rated appliances, low energy bulbs, geezer blankets and/or timers, established electricity strategy such as switching off appliances and lights when not being used.

 **Recycling:** Established policy to reduce and re-use waste, the recycling of any of the following resources: Paper, Glass, Tin, Plastic and Organic Matter, on-site composting and wormeries.

 **Renewable Energy:** Utilising solar and/or wind energy through solar panels and/or wind turbines.

 **Green Design:** Incorporated into the design of the building: proper insulation, sustainable and renewable building materials, maximising light and energy from the sun, building with recycled materials, non-toxic paints and other building materials, water and energy efficiency.

 **Carbon Neutral:** Planting of trees to off-set the carbon footprint of the establishment and its guests.

## EARTH FRIENDLY

 **Eco Cleaning Agents:** utilising or selling products that are fully biodegradable, free of harmful chemicals and not tested on animals.

 **Eco Body Products:** Utilising or selling body products that are fully biodegradable, free of harmful chemicals and not tested on animals.

 **Eco Packaging:** Utilising or selling fully biodegradable packaging and take-away containers made from renewable resources. Accepting returns on product packaging for re-use.

## PEOPLE AND EARTH

 **Biodiversity:** no use of pesticides or poisons, planting only indigenous, conservation of indigenous flora and fauna on your property, alien vegetation removal and rehabilitation of indigenous.

 **Local Products:** utilising products grown or manufactured within a 100km radius, the producing or selling of local products.

 **Organic Food:** Utilising or selling food that is produced using a system that sustains the health of soils, ecosystems and people without the use of inputs with adverse effects for biodiversity.

 **Fair Trade:** selling products or implementing policies which contribute to sustainable development by offering better trading conditions to, and securing the rights of, marginalized producers and workers. Registered with Fair Trade Tourism or Fair Trade Label SA.

 **Empowerment:** Skills development, training and profit share programmes which empower staff and enable better working conditions and work opportunities.

## ANIMAL FRIENDLY

 **Free Range Chicken:** raised in a humane manner with freedom to roam and constant access to vegetation, fresh air and fresh water. Chickens free of hormones and antibiotics (check with your supplier if they meet all these requirements)

 **Free Range Eggs:** chickens raised in a humane manner with freedom to roam and constant access to vegetation, fresh air and fresh water. Chickens free of hormones and antibiotics (check with your supplier if they meet all these requirements)

 **Badger Friendly Honey:** utilising or selling honey accredited with the Endangered Wildlife Trust certificate to ensure no honey badgers are harmed in the production of the honey.

 **Ethically Farmed Products:** utilising or selling free range meat and/or wool products that are have wildlife friendly management strategies which do not include the trapping, hunting, poisoning and killing of predators. Fair Game endorsed products.

 **Sustainable Fishing:** utilising, promoting or selling sustainable seafood from well managed fisheries as listed in the South African Sustainable Seafood Initiative (SASSI).

 **Free Range Pork:** Raised in a humane manner with freedom to roam outdoors and constant access to vegetation, fresh air and fresh water. Pigs free of hormones and antibiotics and their feed free of animal by-products (check with your supplier if they meet all these requirements)

 **Veg Or Vegan:** Serving purely vegetarian or vegan food, thereby providing healthy eating alternatives and decreasing the amount of natural resources used in the production of food.

# SSTL JOINS #IY2017 INITIATIVE

The **Seychelles Sustainable Tourism Label** (SSTL) has partnered with TourismTattler.com in supporting Africa's contribution to the aims and aspirations of the United Nations 2030 Agenda for Sustainable Development, the Sustainable Development Goals (SDGs), and the International Year of Sustainable Tourism for Development (#IY2017).

Launched on World Tourism Day on 27 September 2011, the SSTL is an international concept that establishes a set of standards to encourage and guide Seychellois tourism operators to play a vital role in adopting best practices in the operation of their businesses in order to ensure the sustainability of the Seychelles tourism industry.

The development of the Sustainability Label for Seychelles is in line with a recommendation made in the Seychelles Government's Vision 21: Tourism Development in Seychelles 2001-2010. A study on certification for tourism operators, in consultation with the industry, recommended the development of such a Sustainability Label on the basis of strict, transparent, fair and externally checked criteria.

The label is in line with the UNWTO's call to use the Global Code of Ethics for Tourism to guide tourism development so that they become "sustainable, ethical and responsible".

The SSTL is a sustainable tourism management and certification programme designed specifically for use in Seychelles. It is voluntary, user-friendly, and designed to inspire more efficient and sustainable ways of doing business.

**SSTL Vision**

Every hotel enterprise in Seychelles integrates sustainability practices in their business operations.

**SSTL Mission**

To encourage hotels in Seychelles to mainstream sustainability practices into their business operations to safeguard the biodiversity and culture of Seychelles, by:

- Assisting operators in improving the sustainability of their operations with useful tips and advice.
- Motivating operators to improve the sustainability of their operations by providing them tangible incentives.
- Rewarding through the award of the Label, those operations that have successfully improved the sustainability of their operations.

The SSTL seeks to encourage and guide improvements in sustainability outcomes. As such the project is as much an educational process as it is an examination process.

**What is a Sustainable Business?**

A sustainable business is one that uses its resources today in such a way that the business can continue to be productive in the future. Sustainability is about the natural environment but also includes consideration to the human and economic resources on which future success depends.

**SSTL certified members**

The SSTL is presently applicable to hotels of all sizes. To date, seventeen hotels and tourism businesses have been certified as being compliant with SSTL criteria, which is a third-party assessed, points-based certification scheme that encompasses management, waste, water, energy, staff, conservation, community, and guests.

Commenting on the partnership, Tourism Tattler's publisher, Des Langkilde said "We look forward to featuring each of these worthy SSTL certified properties in future editions of our 'Africa's Sustainable Tourism Gems' series, and to highlight the role that the Seychelles, as an eco-friendly African destination, contributes to the United Nations SDGs."

*For more information visit www.sstl.sc*

PARTNER     SPECIAL FEATURE     SUSTAINABLE TOURISM SOLUTIONS

# Why Join Fair Trade Tourism?

In an industry regarded as being critical to economic growth and development and one that offers such potential for the empowerment and upliftment of impoverished communities and the protection of sensitive ecosystems, it is essential that we have some way of measuring how committed a tourism business is to make a real and lasting difference.

Sustainability is a somewhat overused and much-misunderstood word. Usually associated with being *environmentally friendly*, there is, in fact, a lot more to sustainability than just *green* issues. Most importantly, sustainability means that whatever it is you are doing now you will be able to do tomorrow, next week, next month, next year and for the foreseeable future, without detriment to the planet and with positive beneficiation for people. This goes to the very heart of Fair Trade Tourism as the organisation's DNA has been custom-designed to help people help people.

Through Fair Trade Tourism's Business Development Services offering, a tourism company has the opportunity to unpack its business model and examine it in minutiae, ensuring that every single aspect of the business is optimised to offer real sustainability with demonstrable benefits for communities and the environment.

When a tourism company undergoes the Fair Trade Tourism audit – a gruelling litmus test which comes after the BDS process has been completed – it knows that every part of its business model has been scrutinised and improved upon, using globally accepted measures of best practice in sustainable tourism. It also understands implicitly that it is now ready to build upon the solid pillars Fair Trade Tourism provides it with, which, if adhered to and regularly monitored, will be truly sustainable.

The real testament to Fair Trade Tourism's success is the continued success of the tourism businesses that choose the Fair Trade Tourism route. Their achievements speak louder than we ever could.

So let's hear from some of them why Fair Trade Tourism matters:

### Umlani Bush Camp

"When I first heard of Fair Trade Tourism in 2003 I was excited by the prospects of such an organisation and wanted to be part of it. The ideals and principles that Fair Trade Tourism stand for were exactly what Umlani aspired to be. The certification process gave us new stretches and goals to work towards it also gave us recognition and support for what we were already doing right . This opened many doors for us and put us in contact with many like-minded organisations and people. It has been a magical journey all round and I can recommend joining the Fair Trade Tourism 'tide'. "
**Marco Schiess**, CEO and owner of Umlani Bush Camp.

### Three Trees at Spioenkop

"We decided to join Fair Trade Tourism because we wanted to show our commitment for long term sustainability to our community. We wanted to show that commitment to our guests, so they could be confident in their choice of accommodation and travel experiences and for them to know that the choice they have made has a positive impact on the area they visit. And because we personally believe in Fair Trade Tourism's objectives and principles. We have benefited immensely through various marketing opportunities and networking with like-minded people."
**Simon & Cheryl Blackburn**, owners of Three Trees at Spioenkop.

### Sani Lodge Backpackers

"Fair Trade in Tourism's values reflect the way Sani Lodge Backpackers strives to operate. Having battled with other grading systems, we were delighted to find a certification which recognises factors which we believe are of critical importance in how a tourism business is run. Fair Trade Tourism's criteria recognise our values and reward us for the way we operate. In addition, the rigorous certification and audit process meant that we learnt a tremendous amount about ways to improve and implementing these has led to better performance from staff, more input into our local communities and better environmental practices. We are extremely proud of being Fair Trade Tourism certified and our whole team feels the value."
**Russell & Simone Suchet**, owners of Sani Lodge Backpackers.

For more information, contact FTT Business Development Support at *info@fairtrade.travel* or apply online on at *www.fairtrade.travel*.

ACCOLADES

# Provincial Lilizela Tourism Awards
## Setting the Stage for National Glory

The provincial legs of the 2017 Lilizela Tourism Awards wrapped up at the end of September with the crowning of dozens of esteemed tourism products and services in the country's nine provinces in categories such as visitor experience, tour operators and tour guides, accommodation and entrepreneurship.

It is now all systems go for the fifth edition of the national Lilizela Tourism Awards ceremony which will take place at the Sandton Convention Centre in Johannesburg on 29 October 2017, organised by South African Tourism. The National Minister of Tourism, Tokozile Xasa, will lead the toast to service excellence while honouring the *'best of the best'* among business owners, contractors and professionals working in the tourism and hospitality industry.

"Not only do all these incredible industry leaders do a sterling job in contributing towards making South Africa a competitive tourism destination, they also contribute to the We Do Tourism initiative, which is an inspiring movement that encourages all South Africans to actively play a role in tourism," says Minister Xasa.

Over 500 finalists were selected nationwide from more than 1,600 entries, after which provincial winners in the various categories were named to compete in the national finals. Of the total vote, 80% came from members of the public as well as travel platforms such as TripAdvisor and TGCSA's Tourism Analytics Programme. The remaining 20% was a score from a panel of high-level judges, whose voting was conducted under the strict supervision of Grant Thornton to ensure compliance.

"Based upon the work performed and the results obtained, we can conclude that the judging process of the 2017 Lilizela Tourism Awards was fair and transparent," confirmed Oupa Mbokodo, Director at Grant Thornton.

One of the most exciting categories of Lilizela Tourism Awards is the Emerging Tourism Entrepreneur Awards (ETEYA), which seeks to recognise and motivate black entrepreneurs who operate small, micro and medium tourism- or hospitality-related businesses.

Minister of Tourism, Tokozile Xasa, explains the significance of this category tailored specifically for SMMEs: "South African Tourism is committed to partnering with established players in the industry to help achieve inclusive growth while aiding new players to grow.

"The significance of transforming the tourism industry cannot be understated, as it has huge potential to become a meaningful job creator for our people and a revenue generator for our economy. It is also vital for South Africa to keep innovating and refreshing our tourism offering, to remain globally competitive. ETEYA helps motivate and incentivise outstanding tourism start-ups to continue on their path of achievement and excellence."

*About the awards: The Lilizela Tourism Awards is an initiative of the National Department of Tourism and is spearheaded by South African Tourism aimed at recognising and rewarding the highest levels of excellence in the tourism value chain.*

*See pages 10-14 for all the winners or visit www.lilizela.co.za*

## ACCOLADES

## HONOURING THE BEST OF THE BEST

## THE LILIZELA TOURISM AWARDS 2017

## PRESENTING PROVINCIAL WINNERS

### ACCOMMODATION AWARDS

| EASTERN CAPE | CATEGORY |
|---|---|
| Mafusa Backpackers | Backpacking & Hosteling 5-Star |
| Tsitsikamma Backpackers | Backpacking & Hosteling 4-Star |
| Tube 'n Axe Backpackers Lodge | Backpacking & Hosteling 3-Star |
| Amapondo Backpacker Lodge | Backpacking & Hosteling 2-Star |
| Kingfisher Guest House | Bed & Breakfast 4-Star |
| Storms River Guest Lodge | Bed & Breakfast 3-Star |
| Ruslington B&B | Bed & Breakfast 2-Star |
| Cannon Rocks Holiday Resort | Caravan & Camping 5-Star |
| Dwesa Nature Reserve | Caravan & Camping 3-Star |
| Tenahead Mountain Lodge and Reserve | Country House 5-Star |
| J-Bay Zebra Lodge | Country House 4-Star |
| Ganora Guest Farm & Excursions | Country House 3-Star |
| Pumba Private Game Reserve - Bush Lodge | Game Lodge 5-Star |
| Sibuya Game Reserve - River Camp | Game Lodge 4-Star |
| Amakhala Quaterman's Camp | Game Lodge 3-Star |
| The Sands @ St Francis | Guest House 5-Star |
| Millbury Guest House | Guest House 4-Star |
| FunkyTown | Guest House 3-Star |
| The Royal Somerset East | Guest House 2-Star |
| Oceana Beach & Wildlife Reserve | Hotel 5-Star |
| Royal St Andrews Hotel, Spa and Conference Centre | Hotel 4-Star |
| Hotel Savoy and Conference Centre | Hotel 3-Star |
| Town Lodge Port Elizabeth | Hotel 2-Star |
| Road Lodge East London | Hotel 1-Star |
| Miarestate Hotel & Spa | Lodge 5-Star |
| The Fernery Lodge | Lodge 4-Star |
| East London International Convention Centre | MESE* 5-Star |
| Champagne Events and Function Venue | MESE* 4-Star |
| Coega Development Corporation | MESE* 3-Star |
| The Oyster Box Beach House | Self Catering Exclusive 5-Star |
| Hluleka Nature Reserve | Self Catering Exclusive 4-Star |
| Bartholomews Loft | Self Catering Exclusive 3-Star |
| Welgemoed Chalets | Self Catering Exclusive 2-Star |
| Beach Break | Self Catering Shared 5-Star |
| Thunzi Bush Lodge | Self Catering Shared 4-Star |
| Mountain Zebra National Park Family Cottage | Self Catering Shared 3-Star |

| FREE STATE | CATEGORY |
|---|---|
| Gariep A Forever Resort Caravan Park | Caravan & Camping 3-Star |
| Monte Bello Lodge | Country House 4-Star |
| Lions Rest Country Estate | Country House 3-Star |
| Letsatsi Game Lodge | Game Lodge 4-Star |
| Art Lovers Guesthouse | Guest House 5-Star |
| Lavender Hill Country Estate | Guest House 4-Star |
| Rochilla Guesthouse | Guest House 3-Star |
| Anta Boga Hotel | Hotel 5-Star |
| **De Stijl Gariep Hotel** | **Hotel 4-Star** ⑫ |
| President Hotel | Hotel 3-Star |
| Road Lodge Bloemfontein | Hotel 1-Star |
| Wild Horses Exclusive Mountain Lodge | Lodge 3-Star |
| Lionsrock Lodge | Lodge 4-Star |
| Mont d' Or Hotel And Conference | MESE* 4-Star |
| **Gariep: A Forever Resorts** | **MESE* 3-Star** |
| Maria Moroka Resort | Self Catering Shared 4-Star |

| GAUTENG | CATEGORY |
|---|---|
| Curiocity Backpackers | Backpacking & Hosteling 4-Star |
| Lebo's Soweto Backpackers | Backpacking & Hosteling 3-Star |
| Naledi Backpakers | Backpacking & Hosteling 2-Star |
| Hyde Park Villas | Bed & Breakfast 5-Star |
| Habitat Guesthouse | Bed & Breakfast 4-Star |
| Morulana Guest House | Bed & Breakfast 3-Star |
| De Hoek Country House | Country House 5-Star |
| Oxbow Country Estate | Country House 4-Star |
| Mont d'or Bohemian House | Guest House 5-Star |
| Rivonia Bed & Breakfast | Guest House 4-Star |
| Sunrock Guesthouse | Guest House 3-Star |
| The Palazzo Montecasino | Hotel 5-Star |
| Thaba Eco Hotel | Hotel 4-Star |
| Riverside Sun | Hotel 3-Star |
| Town Lodge Midrand | Hotel 2-Star |
| Road Lodge Centurion | Hotel 1-Star |
| Lanseria Country Estate | Lodge 3-Star |
| the forum | the campus | MESE* 5-Star |
| Maropeng Conference Centre | MESE* 4-Star |
| Birchwood Hotel and OR Tambo Conference Centre | MESE* 3-Star |
| The Warehouse | Self Catering Exclusive 4-Star |
| Nullarbor Cottages | Self Catering Exclusive 3-Star |

| KWAZULU-NATAL | CATEGORY |
|---|---|
| Happy Hippo Accommodation | Backpacking & Hosteling 3-Star |
| Westville B&B | Bed & Breakfast 5-Star |
| Kwalala Lodge | Bed & Breakfast 4-Star |
| Azalea Bed and Breakfast | Bed & Breakfast 3-Star |
| Qabuleka B & B | Bed & Breakfast 2-Star |
| ATKV Natalia Beach Resort | Caravan & Camping 4-Star |
| ATKV Drakensville Holiday Resort | Caravan & Camping 3-Star |
| Days at Sea Beach Lodge | Country House 5-Star |
| Lythwood Lodge | Country House 4-Star |
| Hawklee Country House | Country House 3-Star |
| Karkloof Safari Spa | Game Lodge 5-Star |
| Leopard Mountain | Game Lodge 4-Star |
| Aha Auberge Hollandaise | Guest House 5-Star |
| The Vineyard on Ballito | Guest House 4-Star |
| Gecko Inn | Guest House 3-Star |
| The Oyster Box | Hotel 5-Star |
| Coastlands Umhlanga Hotel | Hotel 4-Star |
| Garden Court Umhlanga | Hotel 3-Star |
| Road Lodge Richards Bay | Hotel 1-Star |
| The Gorge Private Game Lodge & Spa | Lodge 5-Star |
| Three Trees at Spioenkop | Lodge 4-Star |
| Tembe Elephant Park & Lodge | Lodge 3-Star |
| AM 171 Marula | Self Catering Exclusive 5-Star |
| Rockwood Lodges | Self Catering Exclusive 4-Star |
| **Beverley Country Cottages** | **Self Catering Exclusive 3-Star** ⑫ |
| Nselweni Bush Lodge | Self Catering Exclusive 2-Star |
| Casa Ridge | Self-Catering Shared 4-Star |
| Sodwana Bay Resort | Self-Catering Shared 2-Star |

| LIMPOPO | CATEGORY |
|---|---|
| Bushbaby River Lodge | Bed & Breakfast 4-Star |
| Mount Azimbo Lodge | Bed & Breakfast 3-Star |
| Swadini, A Forever Resort | Caravan & Camping 3-Star |
| Summerset Place Country House | Country House 4-Star |
| Fifty Seven Waterberg | Game Lodge 5-Star |
| Phelwana Game Lodge | Game Lodge 4-Star |
| Umlani Bushcamp | Game Lodge 3-Star |
| Meloding Guest House | Guest House 4-Star |
| Vuwa Lodge | Guest House 3-Star |
| Fusion Boutique Hotel | Hotel 5-Star |
| Limpopo Guest Manor Polokwane | Hotel 4-Star |
| Garden Court Polokwane | Hotel 3-Star |
| Palala Boutique Game Lodge and Spa | Lodge 5-Star |
| Blyde River Canyon Lodge | Lodge 4-Star |
| **Timbavati Safari Lodge** | **Lodge 3-Star** ⑬ |
| African Calabash Lodge | Lodge 2-Star |
| Swadini, A Forever Resort | MESE* 3-Star |
| Protea Hotel Ranch Resort | Self Catering Exclusive 4-Star |
| ATKV Klein-Kariba | Self Catering Exclusive 3-Star |
| Mabula Share Block Companies Partnership | Self Catering Shared 4-Star |
| ATKV Eiland Spa | Self Catering Shared 3-Star |

| MPUMALANGA | CATEGORY |
|---|---|
| Matumi Golf Lodge | Bed & Breakfast 5-Star |
| Blue Jay Lodge | Bed & Breakfast 4-Star |
| La Picasso Guesthouse | Bed & Breakfast 3-Star |
| Blyde Canyon, A Forever Resort | Caravan & Camping 3-Star |
| Umsisi House | Country House 5-Star |
| Kaapschehoop Gastehuis | Country House 3-Star |
| Jock Safari Lodge | Game Lodge 5-Star |
| Elephant Plains Game Lodge | Game Lodge 4-Star |
| Leaves Lodge & Spa | Guest House 5-Star |
| Turaco Lodge | Guest House 4-Star |
| McBest Guest House | Guest House 3-Star |
| Schneider's Boutique Hotel | Hotel 5-Star |
| Southern Sun Emnotweni | Hotel 4-Star |
| Graskop Hotel | Hotel 3-Star |
| Town Lodge Mbombela | Hotel 2-Star |
| Road Lodge Mbombela | Hotel 1-Star |
| Needles Lodge | Lodge 4-Star |
| **Hamilton Parks Country Lodge** | **Lodge 3-Star** ⑫ |
| Emnotweni Arena | MESE* 5-Star |
| Badplaas A Forever Resort Conference | MESE* 3-Star |
| Valbonne Villa at Tomjachu Bush Retreat | Self Catering Exclusive 4-Star |
| The Cycad Lodge & Chalets | Self Catering Exclusive 4-Star |
| **Thaba Tsweni Lodge & Safaris** | **Self Catering Exclusive 3-Star** ⑭ |
| Kruger Park Lodge | Self Catering Shared 4-Star |
| Jackalberry Ridge | Self Catering Shared 3-Star |

| NORTH WEST | CATEGORY |
|---|---|
| **Kosmos Manor Guest House** | **Bed & Breakfast 5-Star** ⑭ |
| Boubou Bed and Breakfast | Bed & Breakfast 4-Star |
| ATKV Buffelspoort Holiday Resort | Caravan & Camping 4-Star |
| Tented Adventures Pilanesberg | Caravan & Camping 2-Star |
| Shepherd's Tree Game Lodge | Game Lodge 5-Star |
| Madikwe River Lodge | Game Lodge 4-Star |
| El Shadai Guesthouse | Guest House 5-Star |
| Thaba Legae Guest Lodge | Guest House 4-Star |
| Franka Guesthouse | Guest House 3-Star |
| The Royal Marang Hotel | Hotel 5-Star |
| Protea Hotel Hunters Rest | Hotel 3-Star |
| Road Lodge Potchefstroom | Hotel 1-Star |
| aha Lesedi | Lodge 3-Star |
| Mphebatho Cultural Museum | MESE* 4-Star |
| Rio Hotel Casino Convention Resort | MESE* 3-Star |
| Anne's Place | Self Catering Exclusive 4-Star |
| Monsieur Devan Trust | Self Catering Exclusive 4-Star |
| Mount Amanzi Share Block | Self Catering Exclusive 3-Star |

| NORTHERN CAPE | CATEGORY |
|---|---|
| **@Belurana River Boutique Hotel** | **Bed & Breakfast 4-Star** ⑬ |
| Classic Court B&B and Villa | Bed & Breakfast 3-Star |
| Oleander Guest House | Guest House 5-Star |
| **River Place Manor** | **Guest House 4-Star** ⑭ |
| De Herberg Lodge | Guest House 3-Star |
| Kimberley Anne Small Luxury Hotel | Hotel 4-Star |
| Garden Court Kimberley | Hotel 3-Star |
| Road Lodge Kimberley | Hotel 1-Star |
| Mittah Seperepere Convention Centre | MESE* 4-Star |
| Koekais Guest Farm | Self Catering Exclusive 4-Star |
| Dronfield Nature Reserve | Self Catering Exclusive 3-Star |

| WESTERN CAPE | CATEGORY |
|---|---|
| Saltycrax Backpackers | Backpacking & Hosteling 5-Star |
| Once in Cape Town | Backpacking & Hosteling 4-Star |
| Southern Comfort Guest Lodge | Bed & Breakfast 4-Star |
| Knysna Herons Guest House | Bed & Breakfast 3-Star |
| Dibiki Holiday Resort | Caravan & Camping 4-Star |
| Plettenberg A Forever Resort Caravan Park | Caravan & Camping 3-Star |
| Grand Dedale Country House | Country House 5-Star |
| Hawksmoor House | Country House 4-Star |
| Sanbona Wildlife Reserve - Dwyka Lodge | Game Lodge 5-Star |
| Aquila Private Game Reserve and Spa | Game Lodge 4-Star |
| Villa Afrikana Guest Suites | Guest House 5-Star |
| Avondrood Guesthouse | Guest House 4-Star |
| Afrovibe Beach House | Guest House 3-Star |
| The Andros Deluxe Boutique Hotel | Hotel 5-Star |
| Franschhoek Boutique Hotel | Hotel 4-Star |
| Eendracht Hotel & Apartments | Hotel 3-Star |
| Town Lodge Bellville | Hotel 2-Star |
| Road Lodge N1 City | Hotel 1-Star |
| Bushmans Kloof Wilderness Reserve & Wellness Retr | Lodge 5-Star |
| Kuriguru Lodge @ Tri Active | Lodge 3-Star |
| The Forum | Embassy Hill | MESE* 5-Star |
| Orange Grove Farm | Self Catering Exclusive 5-Star |
| **Petit & Grande Plaisir** | **Self Catering Exclusive 4-Star** ⑫ |
| **Big Sky Cottages** | **Self Catering Exclusive 3-Star** ⑫ |
| ATKV Hartenbos Strandoord Self-catering | Self Catering Exclusive 2-Star |
| Marine Square Luxury Suites | Self Catering Shared 5-Star |
| ATKV Goudini Spa - 4 star units | Self Catering Shared 4-Star |
| Plettenberg A Forever Resort Chalets | Self Catering Shared 3-Star |

⑫ = See page for more info on this listing    * MESE = Meetings, Exhibitions and Special Events.

# PRESENTING PROVINCIAL WINNERS

## THE LILIZELA TOURISM AWARDS 2017

# HONOURING THE BEST OF THE BEST

ACCOLADES

## VISITOR EXPERIENCE AWARDS

| EASTERN CAPE | CATEGORY |
|---|---|
| Untouched Adventures | Action & Adventure |
| Chokka Trail | Beach Experience |
| Miarestate Hotel & Spa | Lap of Luxury |
| Raggy Charters | Marine Adventure |
| Baviaanskloof World Heritage Site | Scenic Beauty |
| Sibuya Game Reserve - River Camp | Wildlife Encounters |

| FREE STATE | CATEGORY |
|---|---|
| Clarens Xtreme Adventures | Action & Adventure |
| Oliewenhuis Art Museum | Culture and Lifestyle |
| Naval Hill Planetarium | Scenic Beauty |

| GAUTENG | CATEGORY |
|---|---|
| Fly S.A. Wise | Action & Adventure |
| SAB World of Beer | Culture and Lifestyle |
| Lebo's Soweto Backpackers | Roots & Culture |

| KWAZULU-NATAL | CATEGORY |
|---|---|
| Big Rush | Action & Adventure |
| AKTV Natalia Beach Resort | Beach Experience |
| Splashy Fen Music Festival | Culture and Lifestyle |
| Karlkloof Safari Spa | Lap of Luxury |
| uShaka Marine World | Marine Adventure |
| Talana Museum | Roots & Culture |
| Midlands Meander | Scenic Beauty |

| MPUMALANGA | CATEGORY |
|---|---|
| Lowveld Extreme Adventures | Action & Adventure |
| Potluck Boskombuis | Culture & Lifestyle |
| Matsamo Cultural Village | Roots & Culture |
| Blyde River Canyon | Scenic Beauty |

| NORTH WEST | CATEGORY |
|---|---|
| Harties Cableway | Action & Adventure |
| aha Lesedi | Roots & Culture |
| Mankwe Gametrackers | Wildlife Encounters |

| NORTHERN CAPE | CATEGORY |
|---|---|
| The Workshop ko Kasi | Culture and Lifestyle |
| The Big Hole | Roots & Culture |

| WESTERN CAPE | CATEGORY |
|---|---|
| AfriCanyon | Action & Adventure |
| Maboneng Township Arts Experience | Culture and Lifestyle |
| Hollywood Mansion Camps Bay | Lap of Luxury |
| Ocean Blue Adventures | Marine Adventure |
| GOLD Restaurant | Roots & Culture |
| Cape Point | Scenic Beauty |
| Ocean Blue Adventures | Wildlife Encounters |

## TOUR OPERATOR AWARDS

| AWARDEE | PROVINCE | CATEGORY |
|---|---|---|
| Imonti Tours cc | Eastern Cape | Emerging |
| Stormsriver Adventures | Eastern Cape | Established |
| Thabile Tours and Shuttle | Free State | Emerging |
| Vuka Tours | Free State | Established |
| Boyang Gape Tours and Travels | Gauteng | Established |
| Bonana Tours | KwaZulu-Natal | Emerging |
| Camissa Travel and Marketing | Western Cape | Emerging |

## TOURIST GUIDE AWARDS

| AWARDEE | PROVINCE | CATEGORY |
|---|---|---|
| David McNair | Eastern Cape | Nature Guide |
| Siseko Yelani | Eastern Cape | Nature Guide |
| Rantseke Rantseke | Free State | Culture Guide |
| Siphiwe Abram Khumalo | Gauteng | Culture Guide |
| Stacey Farell | KwaZulu-Natal | Nature Guide |
| Bongi Thabedo | KwaZulu-Natal | Culture Guide |
| Johannes Outram | KwaZulu-Natal | Adventure Guide |
| Tshamane Isaiah Banda | Limpopo | Nature Guide |
| Mukhena Masilo Gedion | Limpopo | Culture Guide |
| Jaco Buys | Mpumalanga | Nature Guide |
| Samuel Seleke | North West | Nature Guide |
| Mncedisi Thambe | North West | Culture Guide |
| Kabelo Mothupi | Northern Cape | Nature Guide |
| Maruping Kegomoditswe | Northern Cape | Culture Guide |
| George Skaris | Western Cape | Culture Guide |
| Ian Slatem | Western Cape | Adventure Guide |

## UNIVERSAL ACCESSIBILITY AWARDS

| AWARDEE | PROVINCE | CATEGORY |
|---|---|---|
| Access2africa Safaris | KwaZulu-Natal | Experience Visual |
| Access2africa Safaris | KwaZulu-Natal | Experience Commuinicative |
| The Big Hole | Northern Cape | Experience Mobility |

## ETEYA AWARDS

| AWARDEE | PROVINCE | CATEGORY |
|---|---|---|
| Mthombo's Palace | Eastern Cape | ETEYA |
| Fly S.A. Wise | Gauteng | ETEYA |
| Ezulwini Guest House | KwaZulu-Natal | ETEYA |
| Lowveld Extreme Adventures | Mpumalanga | ETEYA |
| Lapologa Bed and Breakfast | Limpopo | ETEYA |
| The Workshop ko Kasi | Northern Cape | ETEYA |
| Afrovibe Experiences | Western Cape | ETEYA |

## MECs AWARD

| AWARDEE | PROVINCE | CATEGORY |
|---|---|---|
| Syavaya Tours | KwaZulu-Natal | Tour Operator's Award |

# Voted SOUTH AFRICA'S BEST

**de Stijl Hotel** offers the weary traveller a perfect stop-over with mouth-watering Bo Karoo Cuisine and a treasure-trove of fine wines! de Stijl hotel offers 43 superbly appointed rooms with breathtaking views of the Gariepdam.

**de Stijl Gariep Hotel**
2 Aasvoel Street • Gariepdam • Free State
+27 (0)51-754-0060/1/2
reservations@destijl.co.za or info@destijl.co.za
www.destijl.co.za

## BEVERLEY
### COUNTRY COTTAGES
attention to detail . farm style comfort . service excellence

Dargle, KwaZulu - Natal Midlands

"At Beverley Country Cottages you'll feel **welcome, relaxed and at home**"

Office: +27 (0)33 940 0972    Cell: +27 (0)82 895 4002
info@beverleycountrycottages.co.za    www.beverleycountrycottages.co.za

This 3-star rated country lodge is family owned and managed with passion and dedication to service excellence. Comfortable and affordable accommodation is assured, along with delicious meals and on-site activities such as 4x4 tracks and hiking trails. Perfectly positioned in the heart of the Mpumalanga Lowveld - the gateway to the Kruger National Park and Blyde River Canyon - Hamilton Parks provides bushveld living at its best.

## HAMILTON PARKS
COUNTRY LODGE

+27 (0)74 252 7037 | 082 723 3722 | 082 836 7360
hamiltonparks.com    space@hamiltonparks.com

## Petit & Grande Plaisir
### SELF-CATERING COTTAGES • FRANSCHHOEK
★★★★

The Petit Plaisir Cottage is 12 years old and the Grande Plaisir was added 2 years ago in the quaint little town of Franschhoek, a fine wine and dining hotspot and one of South Africa's iconic destinations. In fact, there is so much to see and do that it's best if you don't rush your stay. **Petit & Grande Plaisir** is the perfect romantic hideaway for couples who like to tour on their own terms.

Our cottages are fully equipped and stylishly decorated with an understated elegance that has earned us acknowledgement as the best four-star exclusive self-catering in the Western Cape at the 2017 Lilizela Tourism Awards.

+27 (0)21 876 3091 | +27 (0)83 376 9930
petitplaisir.co.za | info@petitplaisir.co.za

# Voted SOUTH AFRICA'S BEST

**Timbavati Safari Lodge** is perfectly positioned just minutes from the heart of the world-renowned Kruger National Park near Orpen Gate. Accommodation for up to 90 guests is provided in 42 traditional Ndebele painted Rondavels and chalets, situated amid beautiful shady trees, and all rooms are en-suite with mosquito nets and ceiling fans. Specializing in group travel, small groups & families and single travelers, Timbavati Safari Lodge offers an array of activities including Day Drives into Central Kruger National Park, Morning & Sunset Drives into the Greater Kruger National Park, Guided Bush Walks & Cultural Village Walks, as well as visits to the various points of interest in the Lowveld. Shuttle transfers are provided to and from Nelspruit, Hoedspruit, Eastgate airport, and the surrounding areas.

## TIMBAVATI Safari Lodge

Sanlam Top Destination Awards: 2017 3-Star Game Lodge Winner

GPS -24.561808, 31.150629 • Hoedspruit • 1380 • Limpopo • South Africa
+27 (0)15 793 0415 • timbavati@mweb.co.za • www.timbavatisafarilodge.com

## Belurana
### COLLECTION - UPINGTON

The 4-star rated **@Belurana River Boutique Hotel** forms part of the prestigious Belurana Collection, which includes the Belurana Victoria Manor in Upington and the Belurana Amzee Mosselbay in Diazstrand. Whilst Belurana River Boutique Hotel is the flagship of the collection, all three properties provide luxurious accommodation in tastefully decorated rooms with world-class hospitality and are equipped to cater for functions and weddings.

Belurana River Boutique Hotel boasts an olympic size swimming pool and serves scrumptious breakfasts on private patios overlooking the Orange River in Upington. Nearby attractions include the Quiver Tree Route, the Kgalagadi Transfrontier Park, and excursions to view the renowned Namaqualand flowers when in season.

+27 (0)54 332 4323 | 054 331 1188 | 086 225 2376
beluranaupington.com | belurana@mweb.co.za

# Voted SOUTH AFRICA'S BEST

Located in the heart of the little Monaco of Hartebeespoort Dam lies the award winning 5-star **Kosmos Manor Guest House & Conference Venue**, where a warm greeting awaits you from the friendly team who are on hand to personally welcome and pamper you from arrival to departure.

+27 (0)12 253 5116 | +27 (0)82 375 0000 | bookings@kosmosmanor.co.za

www.kosmosmanor.co.za | @KosmosManor

25°44'31.69S | 27°50'53.03E

With the mighty Orange River right on your doorstep, spectacular sunsets and star-filled African skies, **River Place Manor** offers an ambience of unequalled peace and tranquillity in the Northern Cape. Situated on one of Upington's wine estates, this exclusive guest house is only three minutes from the town centre and offers luxury accommodation with 12 individually-styled en-suite rooms to meet the most discerning of guest's needs.

Tel: +27 (0)54 332 3102 | +27 (0)82 491 2338
info@river-place.co.za | www.river-place.co.za

RIVERPLACE MANOR ★★★★

Big Sky Cottages is a mere hour drive from Cape Town and offers modern self-catering semi-detached cottages on the foothills of the Mostertshoek Mountain between Wolseley and Ceres, overlooking the beautiful Buchu lands with breath-taking views of the valley. Quality fittings ensure a luxurious stay with easy access to all amenities. All rooms are fitted with queen extra length beds, hair dryers and safes. Fully fitted open plan kitchens, air conditioners, fireplaces, and patios with barbeque facilities are standard in all units, as is free Wi-Fi with TV and DSTV. A Communal swimming pool and Boma complete the picture.

+27713549209 / +27825517022 | bigskycottages@gmail.com
www.bigskycottages.co.za | Big Sky Farm, R43, Wolseley

## ONE VENUE - ALL OCCASSIONS
### WEDDINGS • CONFERENCES • ACCOMMODATION • WILDLIFE

**THABA TSHWENE GAME LODGE** ★★★★

t: +27 (0)82 896 2452
e: info@thabatshwene.co.za
www.thabatshwene.co.za

# List on Africa's dedicated booking portal

**Accommodation**

**Adventure**

**Activities**

**Events**

**Tours**

# Bookings2Africa.com
*Bringing Africa to the World and the World to Africa*

📞 +27 (0)72 224 9971  🏠 www.bookings2africa.com  ✉ bev@bookings2africa.com

## SUPPORTED CHARITY

**THERE ARE TWENTY NAMES IN THIS WORDSEARCH, BUT YOU ONLY SAW ONE. WEAR A LIFEJACKET.**

SUPPORTED CHARITY

BUSINESS & FINANCE

# Market Intelligence Report

**SATSA** – Southern Africa Tourism Services Association

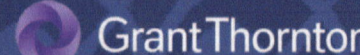

The information below was extracted from data available as at **05 September 2017**. By Martin Jansen van Vuuren of Grant Thornton.

## ARRIVALS

The latest available data from Statistics South Africa is for **January to June 2017***:

|  | Current period | Change over same period last year |
|---|---|---|
| UK | 228 963 | 2.7% |
| Germany | 163 909 | 15.4% |
| USA | 179 002 | 9.6% |
| India | 51 842 | 1.6% |
| China (incl Hong Kong) | 49 285 | -15.3% |
| Overseas Arrivals | 1 295 824 | 10.7% |
| African Arrivals | 3 715 681 | -2.1 |
| Total Foreign Arrivals | 5 017 336 | 1.0% |

## HOTEL STATS

The latest available data from STR Global is for **January to June 2017**:

| Current period | Average Room Occupancy (ARO) | Average Room Rate (ARR) | Revenue Per Available Room (RevPAR) |
|---|---|---|---|
| All Hotels in SA | 63.1% | R 1 244 | R 785 |
| All 5-star hotels in SA | 64.9% | R 2 312 | R 1 502 |
| All 4-star hotels in SA | 64.4% | R 1 149 | R 740 |
| All 3-star hotels in SA | 62.6% | R 942 | R 590 |
| Change over same period last year |  |  |  |
| All Hotels in SA | -0.7% | 5.7% | 5.0% |
| All 5-star hotels in SA | -1.0% | 6.2% | 5.2% |
| All 4-star hotels in SA | 1.5% | 5.8% | 7.4% |
| All 3-star hotels in SA | 0.1% | 3.3% | 3.4% |

## ACSA DATA

The latest available data from ACSA is for **January to July 2017**:

| Change over same period last year | Passengers arriving on International Flights | Passengers arriving on Regional Flights | Passengers arriving on Domestic Flights |
|---|---|---|---|
| OR Tambo International | 3.5% | -1.9% | 1.5% |
| Cape Town International | 25.2% | 3.0% | 2.8% |
| King Shaka International | 8.1% | N/A | 6.4% |

## CAR RENTAL DATA

The latest available data from SAVRALA is for **January to December 2016**:

|  | Current period | Change over same period last year |
|---|---|---|
| Industry Rental Days | 16 936 276 | 7% |
| Industry Utilisation | 71.6% | 1.5% |
| Industry Revenue | 5 294 680 207 | 12% |

### WHAT THIS MEANS FOR MY BUSINESS

Overseas tourism to South Africa continues to grow (see StatsSA data) but tempered demand from domestic tourism (see ACSA data) is resulting in stabilised hotel occupancies.

*Note that African Arrivals plus Overseas Arrivals do not add to Total Foreign Arrivals due to the exclusion of unspecified arrivals, which could not be allocated to either African or Overseas.

For more information contact Martin at Grant Thornton on +27 (0)21 417 8838 or visit: http://www.gt.co.za

**BUSINESS & FINANCE**

# TOURISM BUSINESS INDEX

Mainstreaming Travel and Tourism in the South African Economy

## The Glass Remains Half-Full for Tourism Despite Dip in Half-Year Business Performance for 2017

*Image courtesy of South African Tourism*

The Tourism Business Council of South Africa (TBCSA) has released its half-year Tourism Business Index (TBI) Report, which tracks and provides information about the level of business performance across the travel and tourism value chain, and also forecasts prospects for short-term future performance.

Overall, the industry experienced lower than normal business performance between January and June 2017, recording an index of 82.7 (where 100 is normal). Anticipated business performance for the period July to December 2017 is also expected to be slightly down, recording an index of 80.4. This indicates a slightly less optimistic view of business performance for the remainder of the year.

Delving deeper into the performance of the two main TBI categories – 'Accommodation' and 'Other Tourism Businesses' – actual business performance for the Accommodation sector came in well below normal levels and notably lower than expected with an index of 79.1, compared to the anticipated index of 89.3. Looking ahead, the Accommodation sector expects performance levels to decline further to an index of 66.1 - the lowest level of anticipated performance for the sector since the start of the Tourism Business Index project in 2010.

In the Other Tourism Businesses category, overall business performance also declined to an index of 85.5. However, this is forecast to improve in the second half of 2017 to an index of 91.4. This reflects a below average, but a slightly more optimistic outlook for a segment of the industry that comprises amongst others tour operators, coach operators, vehicle rental companies, airlines, travel agents, retail outlets, forex traders, conference venues and attractions.

Insufficient overseas leisure demand, insufficient domestic business demand and increases in competitive supply are the top three factors cited as contributing negatively to performance. Other reasons cited include the downturn in the economy, increases in rates and taxes and continued water restrictions.

The latest TBI results also correlate with the findings of other industry-specific reports released by Statistics South Africa, such as the tourist arrival figures (looking at a six-month overview) as well as the recently released 2016 Domestic Tourism Survey.

Amongst the positive factors cited is the possible increase in domestic leisure demand, as well as tourist demand generated through conferences and events across the region.

Commenting on the report, TBCSA Chief Executive Officer, Ms. Mmatšatši Ramawela said: "The decline we have experienced recently in business performance has the potential to be temporary if the sector, as a collective unit, takes up the challenge to address the underlying socio-political and economic issues that are affecting business and consumer confidence at a broader level."

**Read More:** Download the Full Report

BUSINESS & FINANCE

# DOMESTIC TOURISM
## Trends & Opportunities

*Image courtesy of South African Tourism.*

South Africa's domestic tourism industry has the potential to contribute significantly more to the economy if it manages to expand the industry so that it caters for everyone in the country rather than just focusing on traditional international tourists.

By **Lee-Anne Bac**.

The domestic tourism sector has provided strong support for the national industry, but it is still only focused on a limited portion of the market by offering the same 'traditional' products to the same type of tourists that have dominated expenditure in this area for the past 50 years.

Product providers assume that their existing products will also appeal to new entrants in the discretionary spending economy, when, in fact, they have very different needs. These travellers are not defined by racial demographics but are rather differentiated by their demand for new and different tourism experiences which are not covered by the current product set.

Factors that influence travel choices for emerging local tourists – often high-earning and high-spending – include family size, value for money, food and beverage options, activities that appeal to their interests, and accessibility.

The 2016 Domestic Tourism Survey conducted by Statistics South Africa shows that domestic overnight trips decreased by 11% over a year since 2015, to 42.8 million trips. Of these, only 7.4 million were leisure trips – a decrease of 13% from 2015.

The increase of 23% for domestic tourists travelling by air in 2016 is encouraging, though this still represents only 1.5 million trips out of the 42.8 million domestic trips in total.

Trips categorised as 'visiting friends and relatives' (VFR) is a potential area to capitalise on. Although these trips decreased by 9% from 2015 to 20.5 million trips in 2016, there is still significant opportunity for tourism operators to tap into, by offering products that would appeal to VFR travellers, or even to convince them to take a leisure holiday instead of a VFR trip.

This does not mean that existing businesses should give away a portion of their market share or products. Instead, there is scope for new product lines and suppliers to enter and expand the market. Importantly, this would also serve to diversify the composition of the tourism industry ownership, which is crucial for the sustainability of the sector.

For the past two decades, we have relied on feeding the informal – mostly crafting – sector into the more formal tourism supply chains, to achieve diversification of ownership and products, but we need more than this.

I see a clear opportunity for small- to medium-sized black-owned businesses – ranging from adventure operators to hotel and resort groups – to grow the available product set and to make the domestic tourism market accessible to more consumers. If the industry manages to grow in this manner, it would go a long way to making domestic tourism even more resilient.

It is critical for South Africa to strengthen the foundations of the local tourism industry, as this provides important support to the international tourism sector. In order to achieve this, all stakeholders need to see the value in the big picture – for the economy – in expanding the product offering, the ownership landscape, and the consumer base.

We need to see proactive efforts from the government by offering more land and space for new entrants, as well as existing suppliers, to allow and welcome new product providers to add products that cater to the underserved audience, without compromising existing supply lines or crowding out 'traditional' tourists.

In conclusion, the local domestic tourism market is ripe for meaningful change which goes beyond focusing on improving B-BBEE scorecards. It is robust enough to allow for expansion that would cater for all types of tourists in different market segments, all over the country.

---

**About the Author:** Lee-Anne Bac is the Director: Advisory Services and Leader: Real Estate and Construction at Grant Thornton
For more information visit www.grantthornton.co.za

BUSINESS & FINANCE

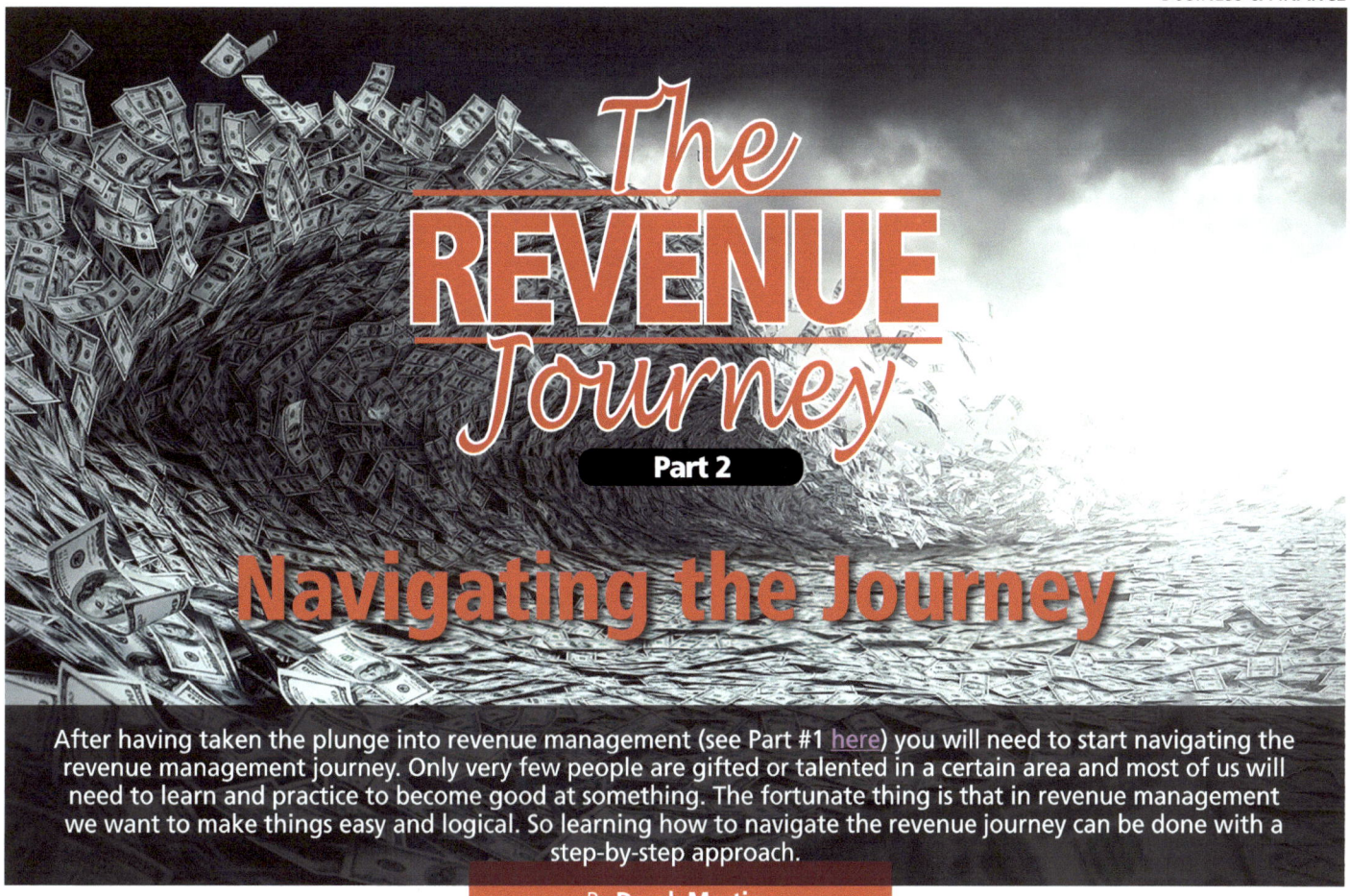

# The REVENUE Journey
## Part 2
## Navigating the Journey

After having taken the plunge into revenue management (see Part #1 here) you will need to start navigating the revenue management journey. Only very few people are gifted or talented in a certain area and most of us will need to learn and practice to become good at something. The fortunate thing is that in revenue management we want to make things easy and logical. So learning how to navigate the revenue journey can be done with a step-by-step approach.

By **Derek Martin.**

## Your situation

So you're the CEO, VP Operations or run a cluster of hotels. And you need to find out where you are in your revenue management journey and where you want to take it.

Whether you operate theme parks, attraction parks, movie theatres, cruise ships, campsites, or of course hotels, you have realized that driving revenue by applying revenue management principles is something that should work for you.

But what are the steps involved in getting the revenue management journey started and going in the right direction?

## Mapping the Journey

As with every journey, there are 3 key questions:
1. Where am I today?
2. Where do I want to go?
3. How do I want to get there?

To find out where you are today you need to ask yourself some questions:
- Is revenue thinking ingrained in all parts of the organization?
- As the first solution to profitability issues do you think about driving revenue? Or do you normally think about cutting costs first?
- Do I have tools in place that help me understand where I am at all times? Do I have a dashboard of critical revenue management information?
- Do I know the speed I am travelling at? And what distance I need to go?
- Do I have the right people in place that can drive the car?
- Am I letting an 18-year-old drive my Ferrari? Do I need to get a better driver?

There is a lot more involved here, but when you look at these questions and you have said 'hmmm' to one or more of them, then you need to do a deep dive into your organization to find out how 'revenue' focused it really is. Being revenue focused is one of the most critical success factors of any organization.

To find out where you want to go can be a challenge at any time:
- Do you want to beat your competitors?
- By how much?
- And beat your budget?
- And be a preferred employer?

The three questions about mapping the journey are not random. In every organization, your customers, your owners and your associates are the key stakeholder groups. And during the revenue management journey, they are all three sitting in the back seat and need to be kept happy. So for each of them, you will need to embed their objectives into your revenue management goals.

All of the above works for many industries. In the next few articles in this series, I will take you through some of the steps of getting revenue management in place in an organized way.

---

**About the Author:** Derek Martin is the founder and CEO of **TrevPAR World** – a hospitality data analytics company that specialises in total revenue management as well as hotel distribution including sales, marketing and social media.
For more information visit www.trevparworld.com

CONSERVATION

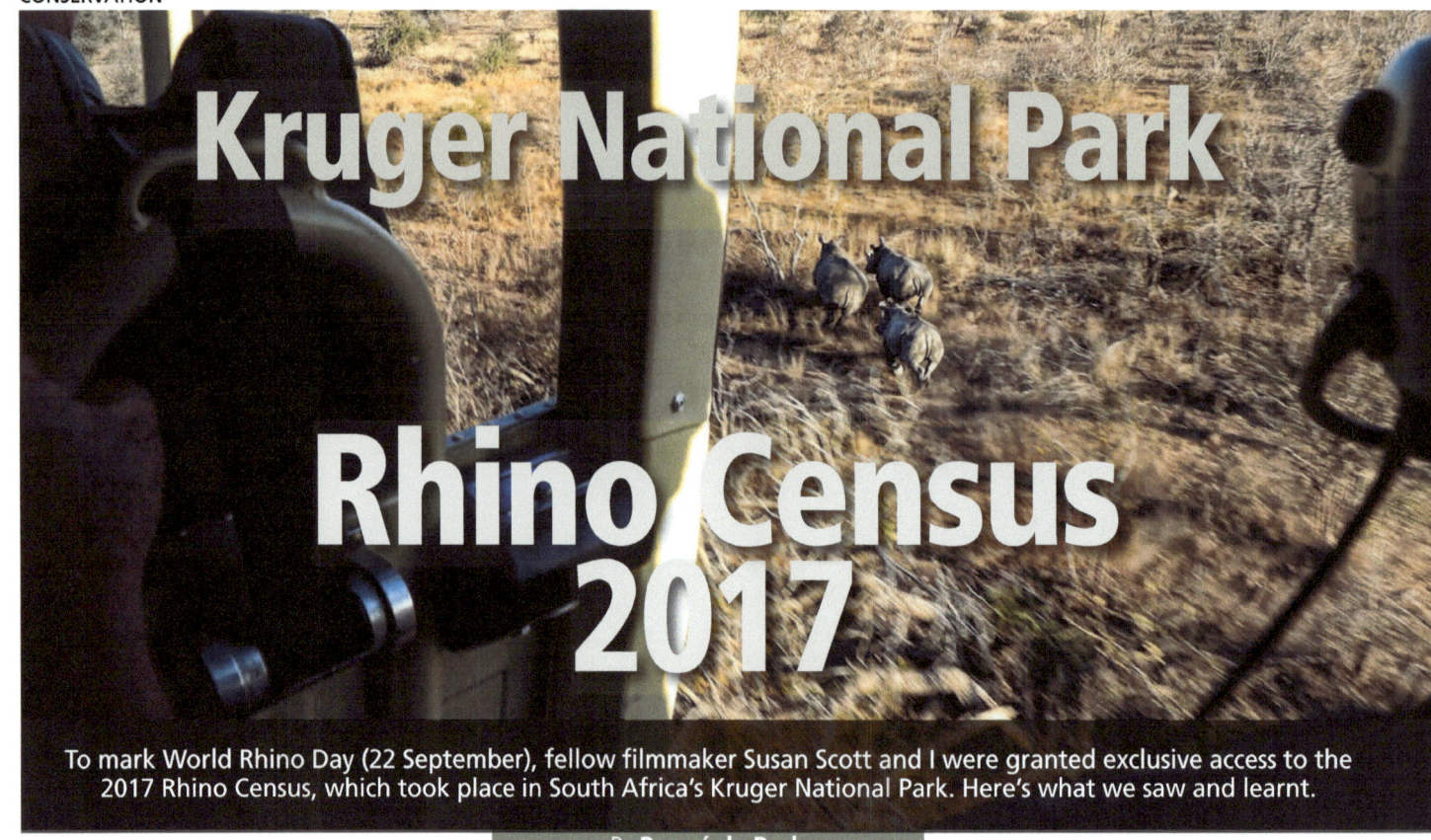

# Kruger National Park
# Rhino Census 2017

To mark World Rhino Day (22 September), fellow filmmaker Susan Scott and I were granted exclusive access to the 2017 Rhino Census, which took place in South Africa's Kruger National Park. Here's what we saw and learnt.

By **Bonné de Bod**.

Susan and I have been working on an anti-poaching rhino feature documentary titled STROOP, which is due for release in early 2018, and we were delighted with this opportunity as it was the first time we had been given permission to observe the rhino census.

### The counting procedure

It was incredible to witness and to better understand the census process. You might think that you go up in a helicopter, count the rhinos and the job is done; but it's a lot more complicated than that. I have tried to observe and film this census count for four years and have begged SANParks every year to allow me to interview the scientists involved and see how it's done.

Obviously, it's a sensitive thing, not only counting the rhinos but witnessing their location and concentrations in the park. I am familiar with census counting of animals but even so, I spent a few weeks going through research papers and scientific journals to try and get my head around the scientific aspect of it all, which was arduous because what it really entails is using a scientific formula to work out how many rhinos there are.

Fortunately, I had the STROOP research team helping me get to grips with it and it did eventually all come together after a lot of reading, analysing and talking to a few scientists. Dr Sam Ferreira is the lead scientist behind the counting of rhinos in Kruger, he is the large mammal ecologist for SANParks and he heads up a team of observers – the people doing the actual counting. So three to four observers in a helicopter do the actual physical counting, and then these results get fed back to Dr Ferreira who uses this set formula to work out the total number of rhinos in the park. Rather complicated but great to finally be able to see it in action after reading all those dry research journals!

### The method and formula

Obviously, a small reserve or farm with a few animals can count a small number by walking or driving around, but in the Kruger, total counts were done up until the late 1990s, meaning that the whole of the park was counted, from top to bottom. But we all know that it's a massive area so you can imagine the time and money that went into a census like that and for some years the census wasn't done at all because of these large-scale factors where the weather had to be perfect. But a total count doesn't mean you will count the exact number of rhinos because a total count will give you a negative bias. You will never see and therefore never count all the rhinos in the park because they might be lying down or walking in the bush line and not observed. This means there are clear errors or biases that one has to consider. So scientists have figured out that it's a far better spend of money and time to do a minimum percentage of the park using a method and formula which they feel give better results.

The specific counting method that SANParks and Dr Ferreira feel is the best for Kruger is called the 'Block-counting method' and the peer-reviewed scientific papers I thoroughly researched, gives a model where you can count between 40-50 percent of the park which will then give a good estimate of actual numbers. So what Dr Ferreira does is to assign various blocks throughout the park which are 3x3 kilometres and then the observers search that block very intensely from the air. Last year they covered 41 percent of the park and Dr Ferreira advised that this year they counted 50 percent.

Also interesting is the flying method. The pilot doing a block-count must fly the blocks in a very structured way, flying narrow strips less than 200 metres apart. When the helicopter gets to the edge of the block the pilot doesn't just simply turn around and fly back close to that strip, they need to fly further away on the edge, worked out to a set number so when they fly back down, no double counting of rhinos happens.

For this, the scientists have also worked in a bias percentage, again done scientifically. But whether you use total or block counting one will never get an exact number of rhinos, and we also have to bear in mind that it's an estimate and even covering only 41-50 percent of the park costs around R1million and that cost doesn't even cover the time of the observers, scientists or pilots.

CONSERVATION

*SANParks Regional Ecologist Cathy Greaver storing information received from one of the observers on board a SANParks helicopter during the rhino census of 2017 in the Kruger National Park. Not only are the numbers of rhino spotted from the air given to Cathy, but also other information such as the sex, maturity and body condition of each rhino. This is loaded into the cybertracker system for detailed analysis after the census count is finished. Image: © Susan Scott*

## Why the census matters

Firstly for management practices, you want the meta-populations (the smaller populations within the total population) to interact, disperse, breed and ultimately grow. Sometimes they do this on their own and sometimes you need to assist by moving rhinos from one area into another within the park system. In order to do this, one needs to know how many rhinos there are at any given time. There is also the need to know and understand the number of live rhinos in the park because of the poaching crisis and how this impacts the population. We cannot just be left knowing how many rhinos are poached - we must also know how healthy our living population is in terms of this terrible crisis.

Many NGOs and activists are questioning the number of rhinos left in the park, and we hear about it all the time from tourists visiting the park who say they aren't seeing rhinos anymore. There also some critics out there, scientists, pilots, vets, who are questioning the number and method used in the park, and many of them say that the number of living rhinos left in the park is an exaggerated number. So quite a contentious issue although not the main reason why SANParks does the census. But they have told me that they hope being so transparent about the counting method used will address people's concerns.

## Conclusion

Rhino numbers have been dropping year on year. Last year's figure was an estimate of between 6 649 and 7 830 rhinos in Kruger for 2016 which was a 16-20 percent drop from the previous year's numbers. These are last year's results, so we still need to wait for the 2017 numbers which are still being collected. We expect the results to be released by government early next year when they do their annual review report.

**About the author:** *An award-winning television presenter and filmmaker, Bonné de Bod, is well-known for her in-depth reporting on wildlife and environmental issues. For nearly a decade, Bonné has presented in both Afrikaans and English on South African television. She has been on SABC's 50|50 for seven seasons and now anchors and produces the popular series 'Rhino Blog' on DSTV's People's Weather. She is also a special correspondent for SABC's Newsroom and kykNET's Grootplaas. On the radio, Bonné updates monthly from the field to Radio Today, RSG and on her program 'RenosterRadar' on Groot FM. For more information connect with Bonné on Facebook, Twitter or Instagram.*

*SANParks Regional Ecologist Cathy Greaver discussing the block counting method with television presenter Bonné de Bod. Image © Susan Scott.*

EVENTS

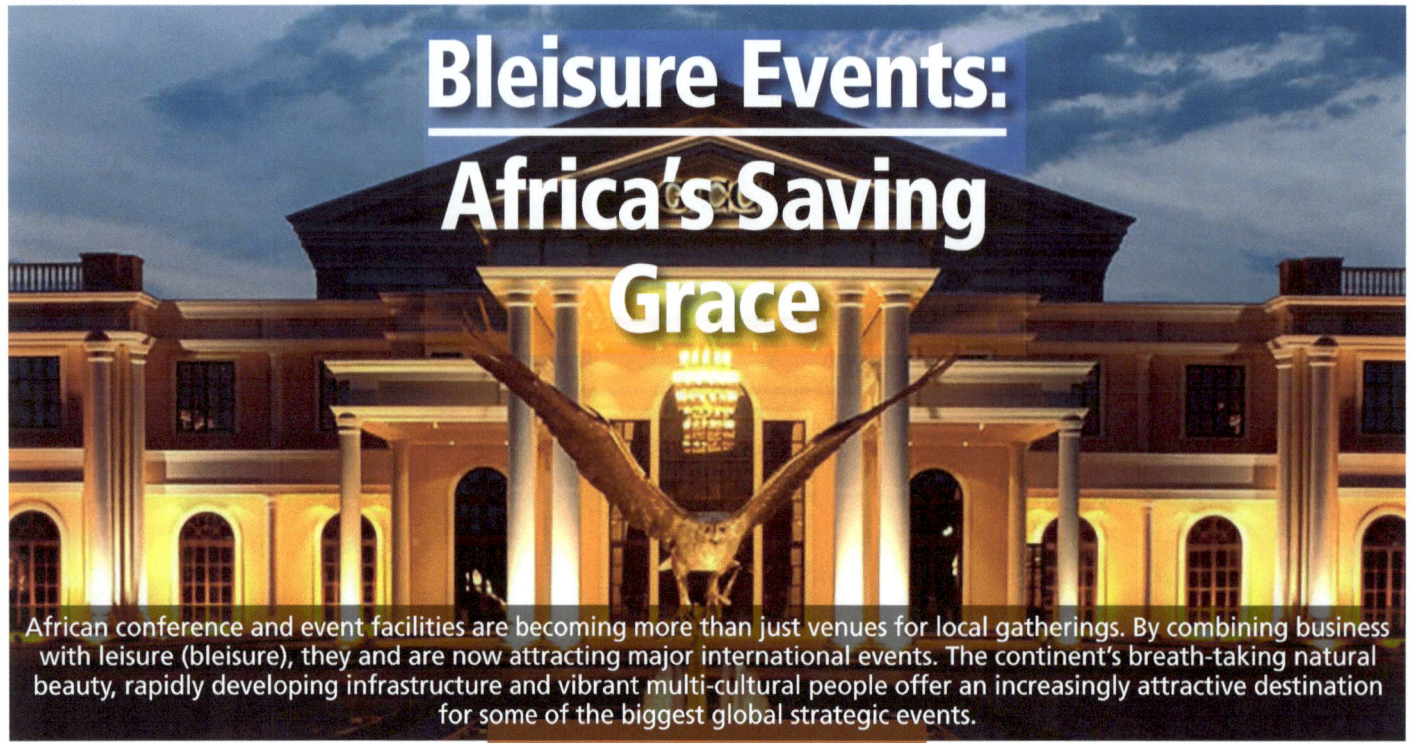

# Bleisure Events: Africa's Saving Grace

African conference and event facilities are becoming more than just venues for local gatherings. By combining business with leisure (bleisure), they and are now attracting major international events. The continent's breath-taking natural beauty, rapidly developing infrastructure and vibrant multi-cultural people offer an increasingly attractive destination for some of the biggest global strategic events.

By **Elzaan van Rhyn**.

With the global economy expected to grow by just 2.7% in 2017 and the African economy by 2.9%, live events have maintained their relevance in a time of cost-cutting. This is despite the potential challenge from teleconferencing technology, which is delivering a much higher image and sound quality than ever before. While the global village is relying more and more on technology to connect people, nothing beats a live event where people can interact with each other for longer periods of time and in genuine ways.

Long-term relationships and contacts can be built without the worry of losing Internet connection or electricity, and nothing could ever replace the subtle nuances of face-to-face contact that are lost even though the most advanced digital contact. Along with a vibrant grass-roots economy, the continent's unique cultural and tourism experiences mean the Meetings, Incentives, Conferences and Exhibitions (MICE) industry in Africa is starting to boom, despite budget cuts.

In fact, while companies and government departments might cut marketing, advertising and promotion costs, budgets are being diverted to conferences and exhibitions, as the measurable return on investment is more substantial and impactful. Increasingly, conference organisers are looking for fresh locations that leave attendees inspired and energised – especially where team building, sales, strategy and creativity are critical elements to the event process.

Global conference organisers also want to host their events at the best locations, where their delegates won't be distracted by the hustle and bustle of big city life. The growing trend towards 'bleisure' hospitality, where companies seek to combine 'business' and 'leisure' elements, is serving to create memorable, informative experiences in stress-free environments.

Developers are picking up on this trend and leading leisure properties are being renovated to include world-class conference centres to cater for business and industry events, along with entertainment. In this way, visitors to African destinations are offered the benefit of sophisticated corporate facilities along with the natural beauty and excitement of the African continent.

There's no better time than now for owners of traditionally leisure-focused assets to boost their conferencing capabilities. While upgrade costs might be daunting, the long-term benefits are immeasurable.

Owners benefit from referrals and marketing their properties while the surrounding economy is stimulated through job creation and new supply chains.

The Grand Palm in Botswana and the Umodzi Park in Malawi are two exciting properties that are attracting people who might otherwise have not even visited the continent.

In 2016, The Grand Palm Resort, located in Gaborone, erected a new multi-purpose marquee to add versatility to the resort, especially for large scale events. Since then it was picked as host to the widely televised World's Strongest Man contest, performances by musician Monique Bingham and the Royal Moscow Ballet, among others.

In 2017, The Grand Palm's four-star Walmont hotel began upgrades to create a world-class aesthetic quality, including a complete revamp of its Okavango and Moremi conference rooms. With new interior design and a full refurbishment of the main conference hall and breakaway rooms, the Conference Centre received a modern facelift that rivals leading venues abroad. With the casino also being completely overhauled, delegates will experience the same standard of excellence across the entire resort.

In Malawi, construction on Umodzi Park commenced in 2009 and was completed in 2012 as a mixed-use facility. It is the ideal business getaway, featuring the 130-room President Walmont Hotel, the only five-star hotel in Malawi. Adjacent to this is the Bingu Wa Mutharika International Convention Centre, which has 15 different venues and the capacity to host 1,500 people in its main auditorium.

The Convention Centre was picked to host events such as the 2017 Miss Malawi pageant and the successful African Land Forces Summit, which received delegates from 44 countries in May, including the US, France, UK, Brazil and leaders from across Africa.

These properties are rare jewels in the African hospitality industry, and as more people enjoy their state-of-the-art features, they will continue to attract interest from global conferences, international musical performances and mega trade exhibitions.

*About the author:* Elzaan van Rhyn is the Groups and Convention Manager at Peermont. For more information visit www.peermont.com

EVENTS

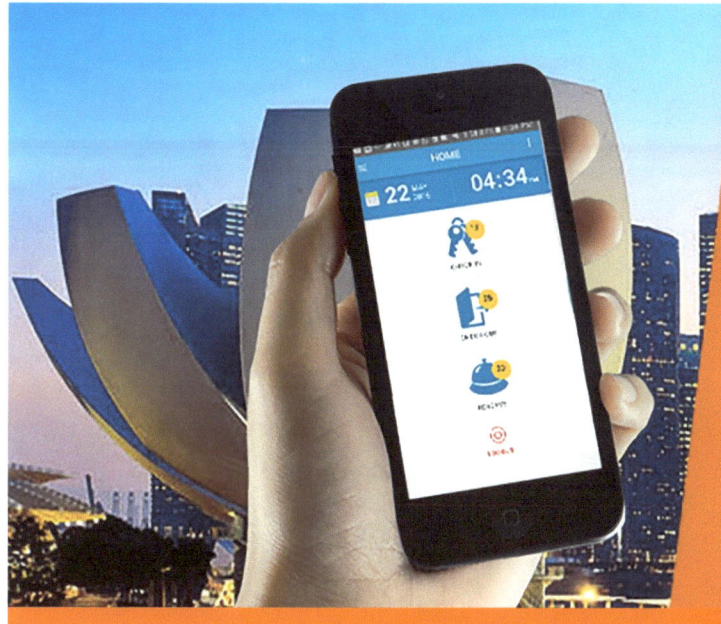 

The Trade Show for the Asian Travel Market

# Hotel App to be Launched at ITB Asia 2017

Being a pioneer in empowering hoteliers with powerful, yet simple cloud-based hotel software to efficiently manage hotel operations, Hotelogix is all set to launch its revolutionary mobile app, Hotelogix Mobile Hotel, at ITB Asia, 2017 at booth B46.

The Hotelogix Mobile Hotel app, that will be available on iOS & Android, has been designed for hotels to efficiently execute, coordinate and monitor operations from their smartphones. Hoteliers can access real-time business insights at their fingertips and make informed decisions on the go.

"Mobile devices are redefining guest-centric services, and Hotelogix is all set to leap ahead of the curve, with our revolutionary new Mobile Hotel app," says Prabhash Bhatnagar, Founder, Hotelogix. "Mobile Hotel is ready, both for the iOS and the Android platforms. Our system puts up-to-the-minute control of a hotel business, literally in the pockets of a smart hotelier. It includes frontdesk, housekeeping and POS that help to significantly improve guest experience, while giving remarkable control on manpower, infrastructure and operational costs," he adds.

### Convenience, performance and mobility

The Hotelogix Mobile Hotel app enables managers and owners to conveniently run their hotels from their smartphones. Frontdesk staff can do away with long queues with express check-ins and check-outs, right from the convenience of the lounge.

Housekeeping information is updated in real-time, eliminating paperwork and enabling tired guests to check-in earlier. Sales teams are empowered to sell immediately, and decision-makers will be able to access a number of reports in real-time, for their hotels. And much more.

"Hotelogix is looking forward to participating at ITB Asia this year. ITB Asia gives us the right audience to showcase our revolutionary products. We are excited to meet hospitality management companies, multi-property groups and upcoming brands to help them take advantage of our simple solution and maximize their business potential," says Aditya Sanghi, CEO & Co-Founder, Hotelogix.

### About ITB Asia

Exploring "The Future of Travel", ITB Asia 2017 will feature industry heavyweights from the travel and tourism sector as well as global brand names from the technology sector.

"As we celebrate our 10th anniversary this year, the substantial growth in exhibitors underlines how ITB Asia has firmly established itself as the leading industry event in the region. The Asian outbound market continues to attract huge interest and we are delighted to see such levels of growth from various key markets at the show this year. While exhibitor floor space is completely sold-out for 2017, we are accepting bookings for the 2018 show," said Katrina Leung, Executive Director of Messe Berlin (Singapore), organiser of ITB Asia.

ITB Asia will take place from 25 – 27 October 2017 at the Sands Expo and Convention Centre, Marina Bay Sands, Singapore. The show is organised by Messe Berlin (Singapore) Pte Ltd and is supported by the Singapore Exhibition & Convention Bureau.

*For more information visit www.itb-asia.com*

### About Hotelogix

Hotelogix is a unique, cloud-based, end-to-end, hospitality technology solution, built to seamlessly manage hotels, resorts, serviced apartments or multi-location hotel chains, by providing a single window to manage all hotel operations and bookings (online and offline). Hotelogix is currently used by properties in 100+ countries.

*For more information visit www.hotelogix.com*

HOSPITALITY

# Floral Cuisine
## ~ Using Flowers in Cooking ~

Floral Cuisine has become a popular and visible food trend in recent times, so in this article, I share some insights, tips and tricks that I've learned about using edible flowers in cooking over a career spanning 16 years.

**By Chef Alicia Giliomee.**

The practice of using edible flowers is as old as mankind itself. Ancient gatherers used roots, fragrant scrubs and leaves (herbs), bark and seed (spices) as well as flowers (known for their pleasant pungent aroma) to draw and infuse in potions. Some were used in ancient rituals and some just for the sheer enjoyment of it, but flowers (just as herbs and spices) have always held some mystical power of adornment.

Normally people aren't sure if the flowers are there for decoration or to be eaten – so, as with any food item, herb or spice, make sure you know if it is to be used for medicinal or consumption purposes. If you are going to eat a flower in its raw form, gently nib off the calyx and stamens which are unpleasant and bitter to the taste. Then start experimenting with different flavour combinations by testing a few varieties. It's like finding a good bottle of wine: the fun is in the tasting.

Use fresh in salads, dressings, creams and coolers. Use dried and draw as an infusion for your favourite ice tea or stir into sauces, jellies and risotto just before servicing for an Avant Garde approach to dining.

I'm often asked why I use flowers in cooking – is it for presentation or taste? I suppose you can ask the same about any other food item for that matter. The question is not what or why, but why not? Our global palate has been subjected to deeper, lingering aromas and flavours. So yes, there is a consideration and misconception with diners that Floral cuisine might not stand its own ground. However, a better understanding of how to use this delicate ingredient will prove that the pretty flower can sing her own aria on the plate (and not just look the part!).

My favourite edible flowers for use in dishes – both main meals and desserts, are the pungent Lavender, Rose, Camomile and Jasmine petals and stems. I use them for sweet and savoury. They pair beautifully with beef, lamb, chicken and even pork. Shellfish stand up well to these pungent petals and pairs well with chilli or a splash of white /rose wine.

Gentle infusions come from the Viola, Snapdragon, Sweet William as well as Wisteria (to name but a few). These petals work well with lemon and can be used for sweet and savoury as well (as in the case of the Pungent flowers).

When it comes to my favourite dishes using edible flowers, one of my favourites is a dish I prepared as *Plat du Jour* at *Die Ou Pastorie*, in Somerset West years ago. It was a Tulip stuffed with White Choc Mousse, with mock Baklava sheets and a Vanilla-Jasmine infused Honey drizzle. Another favourite would be a classic Lavender Bavarois with Raspberry-rose Coulis and Pistachio Melba.

As with most chefs, the fascination of cooking with these kinds of flowers began with a simple recipe for Rose Petal jam from a Margaret Roberts book I read to within an inch of its life in the CJ Langenhoven Library in Oudtshoorn while still in high school.

As to whether this kind of cooking/garnishing is season specific, there are certain seasonal limitations. However, farmers/urban growers have identified a gap in the market and with greenhouses, humidity and temperature control, the demand has been met.

Importantly, when it comes to working with plant matter (as with animal matter), try to use virgin plants/blooms – untouched by pesticides and additional hormones. These components inherently cause a resistance barrier with the cells and it affects final flavour extraction during cooking. You can really taste the difference in the leaf structure – it is coarser and has a slightly bitter aftertaste.

To give TourismTattler's readers a better idea of why I recommend using edible flowers in their dishes, here are some of my flavour favourites:

**Tulips:** Taste like watermelon & dust combined. Torn leaves go great with watercress and chevin (goats cheese).

**Marigold:** Slight pepperiness and a gentle hint of dusty honey. The pepperiness pairs well with Malay-style curries and works well with Beef tartar.

**Hibiscus:** Slight musk & redcurrant flavour. Pairs well when drawn for a tea or made into a tempura.

**Lavender:** Sweet, lingering earthiness with a great deal of tannin. You need to be careful here (just as with a pungent herb like rosemary), for cream/jelly infusions when you need to heat up the lavender, only use the leaves and young stems. The blooms turn the mixture bitter. One such infusion that requires care is Napoleon's Aphrodisiac – basically, a deep and dark hot choc drink flavoured with lavender and a few other secret spices.

**Rose:** Believe it or not, this petal's sweetness is in the aroma. The fresh petal is actually quite bitter. So, when using the petals fresh in a salad or dessert, remember to nip off the white eye of the petal where it tapers down to the calyx.

**Wisteria:** Just like plumbago it tastes of sweet nectar with a slight grape flavour. Great with Brie and asparagus Quiche or turn it into a heavenly jam and serve with scones and clotted cream.

**Sweet Williams** (those mini single layer carnations): Musky pepperiness. Great with Sashimi and ginger. Also refreshing as the heat element in a summer Watermelon & Feta salad.

**Nasturtiums:** Pungent and slightly numbing on the tongue. Pairs well with white meats, fish and shellfish. My favourite is a Salmon and Nastursium Terrine paired with freshly grated radishes and tender stem asparagus.

**Borage:** Derived from the Celtic word "courage", it was traditionally brewed into a tea for the men who went off to war. Now it creates peace on the plate with its deep blue regal petals and gentle cucumber flavour. Too delicate to endure heat-use fresh with Panna Cotta or a Chicken & Duck Terrine.

It's important to note that the type of flower used (as with herb/spice) will influence the listed measures above. Used correctly though, it can contribute to the final composition holistically and not just as window dressing. For example, lavender (as with saffron or cloves) is used sparingly – incidentally both Saffron and cloves are direct flower components (saffron – the stamens from the crocus flower; cloves – the unopened flower buds of a tropical tree).

When it comes to texture, the leaves are delicate, but as with some, you can turn them into tempura/crystallized petals and it immediately turns the tables 180 degrees.

In terms of prepping edible flowers, I recommend rinsing in a light saline solution (salt water to kill or ward off unwanted insects or bacteria), then very gently rinse and shake off additional moisture droplets and place on paper towel sheets. Before consumption remove the calyx with stamens.

Separate from flowers for eating, I also use flowers to decorate.

Whole small flowers can be frozen into ice rings or cubes for a pretty addition to punches and other beverages, which always impresses.

You can also line terrine or jelly moulds with petals. To crystallize the petals, start by lightly brushing with raw egg white and then dusting with castor sugar, then leave to dry and harden. Dry in the windowsill and place in a salt grinder with some Himalayan salt, Pink Peppercorns and garlic flakes for a delicious savoury grind. Or dip the rose petals in chocolate and use as cake/dessert decoration.

In conclusion, as with all herbs/spices, there are two things you need to consider:

1. What is the purpose of the product in the dish, and;
2. at what time during the cooking /preparation/service process to add it.

Knowledge and timing are key, but then again, all knowledge is there for the taking if we want to wake up and smell the roses…

---

**About the author: Chef Alicia Giliomee** is head of department for Professional Cookery at Capital Hotel School & Training Academy. For more information visit www.capitalhotelschool.co.za

HOSPITALITY

# Eat Well, Travel Better:
## The Business of Food Travel Podcast

Launched by the World Food Travel Association (WFTA), the 'Eat Well, Travel Better: The Business of Food Travel' is a series of Podcasts presented by Erik Wolf and Aashi Vel.

The podcasts aim to help you become a better industry professional by gaining inspiration from some of the world's most successful people in the food and beverage tourism industry.

With each episode, you'll meet these leaders and discover their secrets of success, as each reveals the obstacles and challenges they have faced, along with their solutions and triumphs, and you'll take away ideas and inspiration to solve many of the same business issues that you may be facing as well.

To learn more about the show and how to appear on a future episode or listen to current episodes, click on the links below:

**Listen on SoundCloud**
- Soundcloud.com

**Listen on iTunes**
- itunes.apple.com

**Listen on Stitcher** (you'll need to get the Android or iOS app)
- Stitcher.com

**Do you want to appear on an Episode?**

If you work in the food, beverage, travel, or hospitality industry, and have a remarkable story to share, then WFTA want to hear from you.

Perhaps you have overcome a serious work or personal challenge or you achieved something tremendous? Email details about yourself, your professional background and your life challenge or major accomplishment, and a statement as to why you think your story would inspire professionals in food and beverage tourism to help@worldfoodtravel.org

The only requirements are that you have a fast enough broadband connection, a quality microphone, and a quiet place for the interview. The show is a podcast, so video is not required. You can count on spending 15-30 minutes before the interview to prepare your remarks. The interview itself will last less than 60 minutes. Superfluous information, erroneous comments and general chit-chat will be edited out before publishing, to end up with an episode of approximately 40-45 minutes.

### Episode 1: Ari Weinzweig - Sweat the Details

Ari Weinzweig is Co-Founder of the Zingerman's family of companies, which include a delicatessen, bakery, catering operation, family restaurant, Korean restaurant, creamery, coffee store, candy store and a professional hospitality training arm. Ari had no idea the company would grow so large when the original deli opened back in 1982. Now, 35 years later, the Zingerman's companies are a true visitor destination in Central Michigan (USA). Ari talks about how everything got started, his vision, and why sweating the details is important. Check out Ari's books mentioned in the podcast.

Click here to listen to this testimonial on how vision translates to success.

*For more information on the WFTA visit www.worldfoodtravel.org*

LEGAL

# SOCIAL MEDIA & DEFAMATION

## TREAD WARILY! Part 2

**What Must Be Proved & Who Has To Prove It (Burden Of Proof)?**

Before I deal with the Terms & Conditions ('T&C') e.g. Facebook, etc, I think we need to get to grips with defamation and to do so we need to 'unpack' (1) the definition I used in the first article, (2) potential damages (claims) and then (3) the defences.

At a meeting of industry professionals I recently attended the issue of defamation was discussed and what was scary was the misconceptions bandied about: not only about what constitutes defamation but what the defences are, so here we go!

If a party ('A') alleges he/she has been defamed by another party ('B'), A has to prove the following: (1) the statement must refer to A; (2) there must be publication/communication to a third party; (3) B must have the intention to defame A; (4) the statement must be wrongful; (5) the content as such must be defamatory; (6) the causal connection (nexus) between the statement and the damages; and (7) damages (quantum) e.g. loss of customers and the financial implications.

So let's look at each of these requirements that the party alleges to have been defamed must prove:

**(1) The Statement Must Refer To The Person Allegedly Defamed**

This means that the so-called reasonable person when he or she hears the verbal or reads the written communication, must know it is about or refers to the person allegedly defamed. It does not have to refer to that person by name – it can refer to that person by implication/innuendo. The test the courts will apply is an objective one.

This is highly relevant to statements about a group or sector that may by inference include the plaintiff – if the group is too *'too large and diffuse'*, the plaintiff may not succeed. (Refer: www.lawyer.co.za).

**(2) Publication To A Third Party**

This means the allegedly defamatory statement must be communicated by the defendant (B) to a third party and not only to the party who alleges to have been defamed (A) i.e. uttered verbally directly to a third party or spoken so loudly to A that it is inevitable that the third party(ies) would hear it or is published in print media (e.g. newspaper, newsletter), an e-mail copied to various parties or that may inadvertently reach non-intended party(ies) or any form of social media. This means the recipient must know or deduct that the person mentioned, referred or alluded to is (A).

Thus it has been held that *'publication need not be intentional – a person may be held liable even for the unwitting dissemination of defamatory matter'* (McKerron 185). It means you have to be extremely careful not only about what you say but who you say it to, who you share it with and how you share it e.g. marked as *'private, confidential and for the recipients' information only'*.

*'Publish'* means almost any form of communication. It could be a spoken or written allegation or even a non-verbal statement like an image that's communicated to at least one person apart from the plaintiff. Something is considered to be published not only by the person who originated it but also by anyone who subsequently repeats it. Clearly, the liability for defamation is potentially very wide, a scope that reflects the law's investment in human dignity and reputation in particular.

The allegation that someone is a rapist is undoubtedly defamatory in law. Both the people who originated it and those who shared or retweeted it are potentially liable. (Refer: research.uct.ac.za/defamation-law).

You may have heard the terms *'libel'* and *'slander'* – some countries (but NOT South Africa) still differentiate between these two forms of defamation i.e.

- Libel is defamatory statements and/or pictures published in print or writing; or broadcast in the media, such as over the radio, on TV or in film;
- *'Slander'* is an oral defamatory statement.

The test is objective and as stated in the first insert even *'body language or hand gestures'* can constitute publication! (Abrahams & Gross).

Here's a drastic example: Maung Saungkha is a poet turned activist who served prison time over a satirical poem he posted on Facebook in 2015. *'He posted a satirical poem on Facebook two years ago that was deemed by a court to be an insult to the president of Myanmar. The poem named no names, but it colourfully implied that Saungkha has a tattoo of the president on his penis. He was arrested and hauled off to prison, where he served six months for criminal defamation'* (Refer: fastcompany.co.za)

More about this and elements that comprise proof of defamation, namely intention and wrongfulness, in the November edition.

---

**Disclaimer:** *This article is intended to provide a brief overview of legal matters pertaining to the tourism industry and is not intended as legal advice.* © Adv Louis Nel, 'Louis The Lawyer', October 2017.

# MAZDA BT-50 4x4
## Conquering Sani Pass

When TourismTattler was presented with the opportunity of reviewing the MAZDA BT-50 Double Cab, it was a given that we'd choose something that could be considered a challenge – especially when the marketing blurb makes claims like *'chart new territories'* and *'conquer the outdoors in style'*.

By Tessa Buhrmann.

So with challenge accepted, my hubby Daryl and I booked a weekend away in the southern Drakensberg so as to traverse the steep and zig-zagging Sani Pass.

Hikers, nature lovers and four-wheel drive enthusiasts will be familiar with this mountain pass located in the UNESCO World Heritage Site, the uKhahlamba Drakensberg mountain range. Rugged and rocky, this gravel mountain pass is the only direct road linking KwaZulu-Natal and Lesotho – it originally served as a trade route between Himeville and Mokhotlong, and has evolved over the years from a path for pedestrians, horses and donkeys to what it is today.

*Editor's note: According to photographer Mike Eloff's* blog, *the first car to 'drive' up Sani Pass was in October 1948, when an ex-spitfire pilot by the name of Godfrey Edmonds, and a group of local workers hauled his Willys Jeep to the top in over 6 hours, along with a huge supply of rope to pull it up and sleeper wood as makeshift handbrakes. Sadly, much of the road has been tarred since 2006 and according to* Wikipedia, *the final phase of tarring is due for completion in 2019.*

Our journey began in Durban where the BT-50 felt quite at home in its suburban environment, perfect for those carting, carrying and coffee moments, albeit a little large in the parking department for me. Once on the open road though it lightened up dramatically offering a comfortable ride, thanks to the double-wishbone layout with coil springs on the front suspension and rigid axle with leaf springs in the rear, all whilst still retaining a chunky feel.

This chunky solid feel certainly came into its own as we began the climb from the grass-clad lower slopes and rocky peaks of KZN to the alpine vegetated plains and peaks of Lesotho, the Mountain Kingdom. The road up to the SA border post offered ample opportunity to test out the manoeuvrability of the BT-50 as we dodged rocks and ditches – this lower section has a long easy gradient and numerous look-out points. Be advised that this is a 4X4 route only and valid passports, proof of vehicle ownership and insurance is required. The route up Sani Pass climbs to an altitude of 2876 m, and on-route the beautiful Mkhomazana River valley slopes get steeper as the road gains altitude.

# TRANSPORT

**FAST FACTS:** MAZDA BT-50 DBL 3.2L 6AT 4X4 HR SLE

| | |
|---|---|
| Price: | R555 700 (Incl VAT) |
| Engine: | 23.2 litre, five cylinder, turbodiesel |
| Compression ratio: | 15.5:1 |
| Maximum power: | 147kw @ 3 000r/Min |
| Maximum torque: | 470nm @ 1 750-2 500 r/Min |
| Fuel consumption: | 9.7 l/100km (claimed) |
| Warranty: | 3-year unlimited km factory warranty |
| | 3-year roadside assistance |
| | 3-year service plan |

*Image © Sani Pass by Vaiz Ha CC-BY-20.*

▶ Watch the video as we put the MAZDA BT-50 through it's paces on an epic trip up Sani Pass.

The higher one gets the steeper the incline – in certain sections, the gradient is as steep as 1:4 – requiring much concentration and a steady hand. The Mazda BT-50's 110kw of power and 470Nm of torque made traversing the rocky inclines a breeze, as did the 6-speed auto gearbox which had us in the right gear for each situation.

When one gazes over the edge and sees vehicle wrecks dotting the landscape, it is comforting to know you're in a vehicle with advanced safety features like Dynamic Stability Control, Traction Control System, Hill Launch Assist and Hill Descent (great for heading back down again), amongst others. What's more, for true peace of mind, the BT-50 is equipped 4W-ABS, Emergency Brake Assist as well as front, side and curtain airbags.

As the fresh mountain streams and waterfalls turned to ice the relatively mild weather grew icier with a wind chill to match. The final few hundred metres of this epic climb was by far the most challenging with switchback following switchback, each getting increasing steeper, rougher and tighter - all handled with ease by the BT-50 and its auto box. Soon the reward of level ground and the Lesotho border post beckoned, and with taxes paid and passports stamped we proceeded into Lesotho on what is now a really good tar road to experience the icy snow on the higher peaks.

Well, we had certainly charted new territories, and conquered the outdoors… all that was left was to toast this successful challenge with a local Maluti beer.

My final thoughts on the Mazda BT-50?

Definitely still a 'bakkie' but with the finesse and comfort of an SUV, giving great ride comfort no matter where the trail leads.

*For more information visit www.mazda.co.za*

**About the author:** Tourism Tattler correspondent **Tessa Buhrmann** is the editor of **Responsible Traveller** magazine.
www.responsibletraveller.co.za

www.ingramcontent.com/pod-product-compliance
Lightning Source LLC
Chambersburg PA
CBHW040056250526
45473CB00043B/1784